S0-AQD-438

DANCING

Written by
Lynn Trepicchio

Illustrated by
Stéphan Daigle

HARCOURT BRACE & COMPANY

Orlando Atlanta Austin Boston San Francisco Chicago Dallas New York
Toronto London

Dancing is
turning round and round.

Dancing is
tapping with your toes.

Dancing is
leaping through the air.

Dancing is
moving your legs and arms.

Dancing is
listening to the music.

Dancing is
acting on a stage.

Dancing is
something to watch!